Fabric Garden

by
Donna Wilder

Donna on the set of "Sew Creative."

Flowers are such an important part of our lives. Think back to many of the significant events in your life and I bet there were flowers involved. A date to the prom probably meant receiving a corsage or boutonniere, Valentine's Day came with hopes of receiving flowers, we carry bouquets of flowers when we get married. Flowers are often sent during the more difficult times in our lives, to cheer up a patient, or to send condolences at the loss of a loved one. Many times we send flowers to congratulate an achievement such as a promotion, or the birth of a child. Flowers seem to be central to the way we mark the important events in our lives.

People normally associate flowers with spring, but if you think about it we really enjoy flowers all year long. Before any of the early flowers make their yearly appearance I always cut some forsythia branches to force into early indoor blooms. The first true sign of spring at my house is a tiny crocus peeking out through the last of the spring snow. In April, when the tulips and daffodils bloom, spring is in full swing and the summer flowers are just beginning to show signs of budding. Summer is a feast for the eyes as flowers of all colors and varieties bloom from June through September. As the cooler weather approaches we enjoy multi-colored mums, and who can forget about the festive poinsettias at Christmas?

During the cold winter months we turn to thoughts of indoor pleasures. For many gardeners that means poring over the latest seed catalog to decide what they would like to grow in the upcoming warmer weather. I thought it might be fun to offer quilters a way to work on their gardens throughout the dreary winter months by growing a garden full of fabric flowers. I consulted with Marsha Evans Moore, who created the *Fabric Garden* quilt for my television show Sew Creative, and together we came up with the twelve designs you will find in this book. In addition, to show the versatility of these patterns, Marsha designed four additional pieces based on several of these blocks.

I would like to thank Springs Industries for generously providing the *Quilters Only* fabric used in the Fabric Garden quilt and accessory pieces. I would also like to thank the following companies for their support of my public television show, Sew Creative which featured this quilt in its 1100 series: American Quilter's Society, Better Homes & Gardens Crafts Group, Gammill Quilting Machine Company, Janome/New Home Sewing Machine Company, P & B Textiles, Quilter's Newsletter Magazine, Springs Industries, Sulky of America, and Wrights. A big thank you is also sent to Laura Reinstatler who checked this book for technical accuracy.

In addition, I would like to thank all of the loyal viewers of Sew Creative. I will continue to bring you craft and quilt projects, hints and tips, and guests from the best companies in the industry. I hope you will enjoy all of the items we present to you and will continue to watch Sew Creative for many years to come.

Donna Wild

P.S. If *Sew Creative* is not currently available in your area, please call your local public television station and request that they run it. It is available at no charge to them and we will be happy to send stations information upon request. Please tell them to direct their requests to: *Sew Creative*, PO Box 2254, Danbury, CT 06813.

Fabric Garden

Table of Contents

Published by: FPC Media, P. O. Box 1130, Danbury, CT 06813.

Managing Editor: Patty Bailey
Technical Editor: Laura Reinstatler
Cover Design: Mary Beth Mason
Type and Graphics: Mimi and John Shimp, SPPS, Inc.
Photography: Brad Stanton Photography

ISBN: 0-9655270-3-4

We have made every effort to ensure that the instructions in this book are accurate and complete. We cannot, however, be responsible for human error, typographical mistakes or variations in individual work.

Materials Needed

Approximate Size: 56" x 70"

Materials

NOTE: All fabrics are 45" wide cotton

2⅛ yards multicolored floral print for border

1⅜ yards teal print for sashing

¼ yard rose

½ yard rose print

⅛ yard rose floral print

⅛ yard dusty pink

¼ yard pink print

⅜ yard blue

⅜ yard blue floral print

⅛ yard lavender

¼ yard purple

¼ yard purple print

¼ yard purple floral print

¼ yard teal green

¼ yard dusty green

¼ yard light green

⅛ yard green print

½ yard black

⅛ yard gold print

⅛ yard or 6" x 4" piece light yellow

4½ yards backing fabric

1 yard binding fabric

four ½" diameter pink buttons

freezer paper

thread to match fabrics

invisible thread

1 yard paper-backed fusible web

acrylic ruler with 45° lines marked

batting – (Quilt pictured used Poly-fil® Low-Loft®.) If you prefer cotton you may wish to use Soft Touch® Cotton Batting.

General Instructions

CHOOSING THE FABRIC

Most quilters prefer to work with 100% cotton fabric. There is less distortion with cotton, which means smaller pieces fit together more easily. Because of the need to press frequently when piecing, cotton is the best choice since it irons flat. When quilting by hand, your needle will move through cotton fabric with ease.

It is a good idea to check your fabric for colorfastness by washing it in warm water before you begin your quilt. Fabric that continues to bleed after washing should not be used. Washing the fabric will also insure that it is totally preshrunk.

SUPPLIES

In addition to the materials listed above, you will need other tools to complete your quilt:

SHARP SCISSORS – used for fabric cutting only.

SCISSORS, SINGLE EDGE RAZOR, OR CRAFT KNIFE – used to cut the template material.

ROTARY CUTTER, ACRYLIC RULER AND MAT – used when cutting strips, squares and rectangles for strip piecing.

QUILTING THREAD – is stronger than standard sewing thread and is used for hand quilting.

INVISIBLE NYLON THREAD – is used as the top thread when machine quilting.

NEEDLES – in size 14 for machine piecing; size 7-8 for hand piecing; for embroidery use size 7 or 8 sharp or embroidery needles.

STRAIGHT PINS

MARKING PEN OR PENCIL – to mark the quilting designs onto fabric. Test any marking pen to be sure that it will not run when wet and can be washed out or erased. A #2 lead pencil may also be used.

IRONING BOARD AND IRON – for pressing your seams as you piece. A steam iron is preferable, but some quilters prefer a dry iron with a damp cloth.

SAFETY PINS – in size #1 or #2 are used to baste your quilt before quilting, unless you thread baste. Place pins no more than 4" to 6" apart, and avoid seams and other areas where you will be stitching.

TEMPLATES

Templates for the pattern pieces are found on pages 26-32. The templates DO NOT INCLUDE SEAM ALLOWANCES. Trace template patterns carefully onto the template plastic. Be sure to include all markings when tracing your templates as these are important for accurate piecing. The templates included are for hand or machine piecing. If you are machine piecing, add ¼" seam allowances to templates BEFORE cutting fabric. Those who hand piece usually mark on seam line and add the seam allowance as they are cutting the fabric pieces.

FINISHING THE QUILT

As you piece the blocks it is important to press seams in opposite directions so that they butt against each other and do not create "bumps" in the seams. After piecing the blocks, they *should* measure 12½" square. Yours may be slightly larger or smaller, but as long as they are consistently the same size, don't panic! Trim all blocks to the same size, and as long as the blocks are square, you will be fine.

Press completed blocks with a steam iron to smooth any wrinkles and make them very flat. Do not iron as you would for clothing – a gentle pressing of the iron is what you want. Arrange the blocks as in the photograph on the cover, or in any order that pleases you.

SASHING: Before joining the blocks, you will need to cut sashing strips. Cut 9 strips 2½" x 12½" (or the size of your block). Join these sashing strips to the blocks as shown in Sashing Figure 1 below.

Sashing Figure 1.

The length of your quilt should measure approximately 54½". Cut 4 strips 2½" x 54½" (or length of your quilt). Add these strips between the vertical rows of blocks and on each side of the quilt. Cut 2 strips 2½" x 44½" (or width of your quilt) and add to the top and bottom of the quilt top. Refer to Sashing Figure 2 below.

Sashing Figure 2.

BORDERS: The *Fabric Garden* quilt has 6" wide border strips. Cut 2 strips 6½" x 44½" (or the width of your quilt) and join to the the top and bottom of the quilt top. Cut 2 strips 6½" x 70½" (or the length of your quilt) and join to the sides of the quilt top. See Border Figure 1 on the next page.

LAYERING THE QUILT: Many types of batting are available for use in your quilt, both polyester and 100% cotton varieties. Choose the type you like best. It is a good idea to open the batting and let it breathe for a day before you layer your quilt. Cut batting at least 2" larger than the top, all the way around.

Fabric for your backing should be 100% cotton, the same as the quilt top fabric. This should be pre-shrunk and pressed before layering with the batting and top. Unless you have 72" wide fabric you will need to piece lengths of fabric to fit your quilt, as it is larger than the width of the fabric. Cut the selvages from the backing fabric. Cut the fabric crossgrain into two 2¼ yard pieces and seam together lengthwise. Press seams open flat. Cut the backing fabric at least 2" larger than the quilt top all the way around.

Border Figure 1.

THREAD BASTING THE QUILT: Place backing wrong side up on a flat surface. Place batting on top of the backing, then the quilt top right side up and pin to secure. Baste the three layers together with long stitches starting in the center and working toward the edges. Check to see that grain lines on top and backing remain even as you baste.

PIN BASTING THE QUILT: Use #1 or #2 rust proof safety pins for pin basting. Lay the backing wrong side up on a flat surface, then the batting, then the quilt top, right side up. Begin pin basting in the center of the quilt, working out to the edges. Place pins about 4" to 6" apart, being careful not to place a pin where you want to stitch.

QUILTING: The *Fabric Garden* quilt was quilted "in the ditch" fashion as shown at right. Quilt along the seam lines between the blocks and along

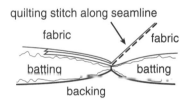

the seam lines of the borders. Quilt along the seam lines of the patchwork pieces and around the appliqué shapes.

BINDING: Cut binding strips 3½" x 45". Sew the short ends of the strips together to make

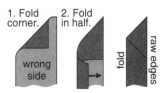

one long strip. Fold raw edge on short side diagonally, then fold the strip in half wrong sides together to form the binding and press.

Line up the raw edges of the quilt front and the doubled raw edge of the binding and sew around the quilt beginning at the center bottom edge using ½" seam allowance.

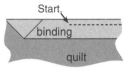

As you approach a corner, stop ½" seam allowance away from the raw edge.

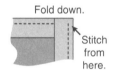

Fold the binding strip up as shown so that you have a 45° angle.

Fold the binding strip straight down making sure the raw edges of the binding are even with the raw edges of the quilt. Begin stitching ½" (seam allowance) away from the folded edge of the binding. (The stitching should meet but not overlap at the corners.)

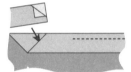

As you approach the starting point, tuck the end of the binding strip inside the folded section as shown and complete the stitching.

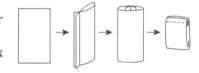

Roll the binding to the back of the quilt and hand stitch in place being sure to cover machine stitching.

HANGER: Make hanging tabs using leftover scraps of fabric. Cut three fabric strips 3" x 5". With right sides together, seam long side. Turn right side out to create a tube and press with seam open and centered on the back side. Fold in half with seam sides together turning raw edges under ¼" and stitch across as shown.

Position the hangers evenly spaced across the top of the back of the quilt (just low enough so that they cannot be seen from the front of the quilt.) Attach to the back of the quilt using hand stitching through only the backing fabric.

Lily

Technique: Piecing Diamonds
Templates are found on page 30.

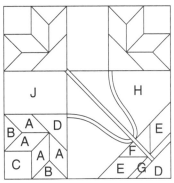

Cutting

1. Make templates for pattern pieces.

2. Cut 6 small diamonds (A) from each dusty pink and pink print.

3. From off white, cut 6 small triangles (B), three squares (C), 2 rectangles (J) 3½" x 5", and one each of sections H, F, and G.

4. From dusty green print, cut 3 large triangles (D) and 2 large diamonds (E). From dusty green cut 1 large triangle (D), one 1" x 8" bias strip, and one 1" x 12" bias strip.

Directions

1. Sew each dusty pink small diamond (A) to a pink print diamond beginning at edge of center point and ending at side corner of stitching line. For 3 pairs, place print diamond on top. For remaining pairs, place dusty pink diamond on top. Trim seam allowance at center point of diamonds. Press seam allowance toward dusty pink diamond.

2. Pin a small triangle (B) between the points of each diamond pair matching side corner of diamond to corner of seam line on triangle. Stitch beginning at inner edge of seam line on corner point and ending at outer edge of fabric. Press seams toward diamonds.

3. Sew two pairs of diamonds together joining them as in step 1. Match pink print diamonds in center to make 2 lilies. Match dusty pink diamonds in center to make 1 lily. Trim seam allowance at center point of diamonds.

4. In the same manner as for setting in triangles, pin a square (C) between the points of diamonds matching side corner of diamond to corner of the seam line on the square. Stitch beginning at

inner edge of seam line on corner point and ending at outer edge of fabric. Press toward diamonds.

5. Stitch a large dusty green print triangle (D) to corner of lilies to make a square.

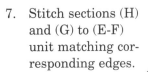

6. Stitch large diamonds (E) to sides of section (F).

7. Stitch sections (H) and (G) to (E-F) unit matching corresponding edges.

8. Fold stems in half lengthwise and stitch ¼" from fold. Trim seam allowance to ¹⁄₁₆"and press. Pin 12" bias strip along curved stem. Slipstitch in place. Pin 8" bias strip along straight stem. Slipstitch in place.

9. Stitch dusty green large triangle (D) to edge of section (G) to form a square.

10. Arrange lilies, rectangles and stem section (D-H) as shown in piecing diagram. Join pieces as shown in piecing diagram below.

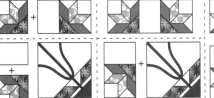

Dahlia

Technique: Curved Hand Piecing
Templates are found on page 29 and below.

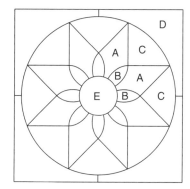
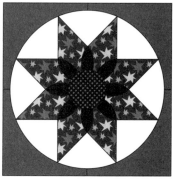

Cutting

1. Make templates for pattern pieces provided on page 29. The template piece shown on this page INCLUDES seam allowance.

2. Cut 8 large petals (A) from blue floral print. Cut 8 small petals (B) from purple. Cut 8 outer circle sections (C) from off white.

3. Cut a 12½" square from blue. Trace template (D) to each corner. Cut out center.

4. Trace center circle (E) to dull side of freezer paper. Cut out circle. Fuse paper to wrong side of gold print. Trim fabric ¼" from outer edge of paper.

Directions

1. Clip seam allowance along curved edges of large petals (A). Stitch a large petal to a small petal matching one curved edge. Begin stitching at end of seam

line at point and stitch to end of fabric at center.

2. Stitch another small petal to other curve of large petal. Continue joining small and large petals in the same manner until all petals are joined. Stitch small and large petals together at ends to form a circle.

3. Stitch a section (C) piece between each pair of large petals beginning stitching

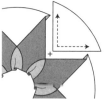

at end of seam line of inner point and continuing to outer edge.

4. Gather center seam line of petals using a running stitch. Draw up gathers so circle lays flat.

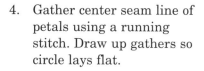

5. Turn under fabric edges of gold print center along edge of paper and baste edge in place. Slipstitch center to center of petals.

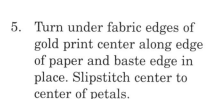

6. Using matching thread, stitch along inner seam

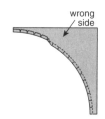
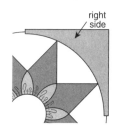

line of blue corner. Clip seam allowance to stitching. Press under inner edge along stitching. Place corner around flower and slipstitch seam lines together.

NOTE: This template includes ¼" seam allowance.

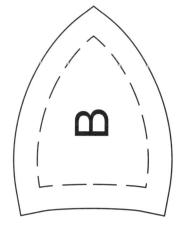

Tulips

Technique: Strip Piecing
Templates found on page 30.

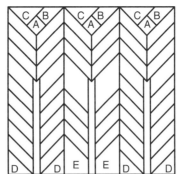

Cutting

1. Cut two 1" square centers (A) from lavender and one 1" center from dusty pink.

2. Cut one 1¼" wide strip across the entire width of the following fabrics: purple, purple print and purple floral print, bright rose, rose print and rose floral print. Cut each strip in half to make strips about 20-22" long.

3. From white, cut one 1½" wide strip across the entire width of fabric. Cut one 2¼" wide strip and three 1¼" wide strips in same manner. From off white cut three each of sections B and C. Cut four triangles (D) and two pieces (E).

4. Cut three 1¼" wide strips from teal and two 1¼" wide strips from dusty green. Cut two ⅞" x 7½" stems from teal and one stem from dusty green.

Strip Piecing Directions

1. Arrange purple solid and print strips into two color combinations of 3 strips each. Stitch each group of 3 strips together. Press seams.

2. Arrange rose solid and print strips into two color combinations of 3 strips. Stitch each group of 3 strips together. Press seams.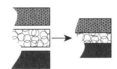

3. Cut two 2½" wide diamonds from each purple strip at a 45° angle. Cut one 2½" wide diamond from each rose strip at a 45° angle.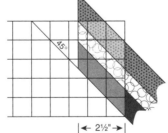

4. Stitch 3 teal strips and two white strips together alternating colors. Stitch a 1½" wide white strip to top edge.

5. Cut two 2¼" wide leaf pieces at a 45° angle, then cut in the same manner as you did for the diamonds in step 3.

6. Stitch 2 dusty green strips to each side of a 1¼" wide white strip. Stitch a 2¼" wide white strip to one side of the teal strips.

7. Cut a 2¼" wide leaf piece at a 45° angle, and another 45° angle piece in the opposite direction.

Directions

1. Stitch each center (A) to piece (B). Then stitch (A-B) to (C) to make a triangle.

2. Matching colors stitch tulip diamonds together in pairs beginning at edge of center point and ending at side corner of stitching line. Be sure to match seams of strips.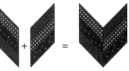

3. Matching colors, pin top triangle (A-C) between the points of each diamond pair matching side corner of diamond to corner of seam line on triangle. (Follow steps 2-3 of Lily block, page 7 for piecing instructions). Press seams toward diamonds.

4. Stitch white triangles (D) to lower edges of teal leaf strips. Stitch white (E) pieces to lower edges of dusty green leaf strips.

5. Stitch leaf sections to opposite edges of stems matching colors. Clip top edge of stem into a v shape. Make a row of reinforcing stitches along center of top seam line. Clip to center of v. Beginning at center, stitch teal leaf sections to purple tulips and dusty green leaf section to rose tulip. (Refer to Lily block steps 2-3 for setting-in piecing instructions.)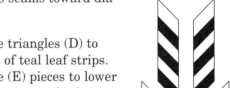

6. Stitch a purple tulip to each side of rose tulip to make square.

9

Urn with Flowers

Technique: Appliqué, Ruching
Templates found on page 11 and 27.

Cutting

1. Cut a 12½" square from off-white fabric. To trace the appliqué design onto your background fabric, make a pattern as follows: Draw a 12" square on paper and mark the vertical center. Trace 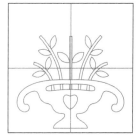 urn, stems and leaves to half of the square. Fold pattern along center and trace design to other half of square. Trace this design onto your fabric.

2. Trace urn, 2 calyxes, 8 small leaves and 2 large leaves to freezer paper. Cut out shapes. Fuse urn to purple print. Fuse 4 small leaves and large leaves to teal green. Fuse 4 small leaves to dusty green. Fuse calyxes to teal green print. Cut out fabric ³⁄₁₆" larger than paper patterns. Turn under fabric along edges of paper and baste them in place. Clip curved edges as needed for smooth turning.

3. Cut three 1" wide bias strips that are 8" long from teal and two 6" long from dusty green.

4. Trace 4 large and 8 small rose petals to dusty pink leaving room for seam allowance around each one. Place dusty pink fabric on top of rose fabric. Pin layers together at center of each petal. Cut out adding ³⁄₁₆" seam allowance.

5. From rose print, cut two 1⅛" wide bias strips that are about 30" long.

6. Cut two 4½" x 1¾" rectangles from blue.

Directions

1. Fold stems in half lengthwise and stitch ¼" from fold. Trim seam allowance to ¹⁄₁₆". Press.

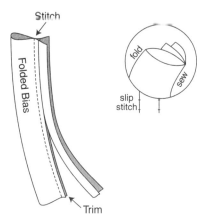

Stitch

Folded Bias

Trim

fold
sew
slip stitch

1. Pin teal stems along center and side stems. Slipstitch in place. Pin dusty green stems along remaining stems.

2. Pin leaves to position along stems, matching colors. Slipstitch edges. Pin urn in place and slipstitch edges. Whipstitch along inner curves to hold fabric in place securely.

4. Stitch dusty pink and rose petals together along drawn line leaving a small opening for turning. Clip seam allowance and turn right side out. Slipstitch edges of openings together.

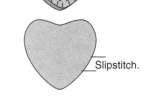

Clip.

Leave open.

Slipstitch.

5. Draw a 2½" diameter circle at top of center stem. Arrange small petals around the circle so they overlap, and sew them in place.

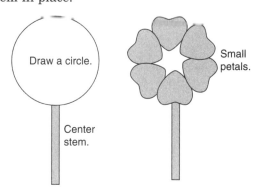

Draw a circle.

Center stem.

Small petals.

6. For rose center, fold upper curves of one large petal to rose side and tack curves in place. Fold sides to center.

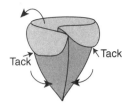

Place in the center of another large petal. Gather back petal slightly around bud and tack so it is three dimensional.

7. Fold points of heart toward rose side on remaining 2 petals and tack in place. Make a row of gathering stitches.

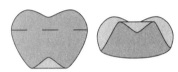

Gather each petal slightly and place around on each side of center around lower edge. Sew petals in place.

8. Sew rose center to center of small petals.

9. Turn under ⅛" on one long edge and short ends of blue rectangles. Fold and press to make 5 even pleats so that flower fans slightly.

10. Pin rose to end of teal stem and pleated flowers and calyxes at end of dusty green stems. Slipstitch.

11. Fold rose print bias strips in half lengthwise, right side out and lightly press fold. Open fold with right side down and press lightly so fold still shows. Fold edges to center and press in place to make a piece of bias tape.

First fold.

12. Make a row of gathering stitches that zigzag along each rose print bias strip following the grain of the fabric. Or fold at right angles to mark diagonal lines, then stitch along folds. Draw up gathers to form petals.

13. Using a second needle and thread, gather lower portion of the first 5 petals to form center, at right. Tack center together. Continue gathering bias tape to make petals that spiral out around center and tack lower edge of petals in place on back.

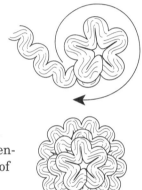

Sew to ends of side stems.

14. From wrong side, cut out background fabric behind urn and leaves, about ¼" inside stitching line. Remove freezer paper templates.

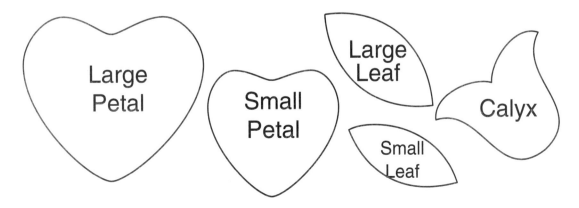

Large Petal

Small Petal

Large Leaf

Small Leaf

Calyx

Grandmother's Flowers

Technique: English Paper Piecing
Templates found on page 31.

Cutting

1. Cut a 12½" x 4½" rectangle from light blue. Cut 12½" x 2" rectangles from each dusty green print and dusty green. Cut a 12½" x 2½" rectangle from light green print. Cut a 12½" x 3½" rectangle from light green.

2. Make a hexagon template. Cut 21 hexagons from freezer paper. Pin 1 hexagon (with shiny, waxy side up) to the wrong side of each blue, purple and rose fabric. Cut out each hexagon adding ³⁄₁₆" seam allowance around each edge of paper. Pin 6 hexagons to each purple floral print, blue floral print and rose floral print. Cut out fabric about ³⁄₁₆" from edge of paper.

3. Make small and large leaf templates. Cut 1 small and 5 large leaves from freezer paper. Pin 1 large and 1 small leaf, shiny side up, to teal fabric. Pin remaining leaves to teal floral print fabric. Cut out each leaf adding ³⁄₁₆" seam allowance around each edge of paper.

4. Place hexagons and leaves paper side up, on ironing board. Carefully press seam allowance over edge of paper one side at a time. Seam allowance of fabric will stick to the waxy side of the paper eliminating the need to baste under edges.

5. Cut two 1½" wide bias strips 8" long for stems.

Directions

1. Stitch rectangles together in the following order to make a square: light blue, dusty green print, dusty green, light green print and light green.

2. Place one floral print hexagon along one edge of the matching solid hexagon center. Join the two hexagons using tiny whipstitches. Place another hexagon along adjacent edge of the pair and whipstitch. Continue working around center until all hexagons are joined. Stitch first hexagon to last hexagon. Make purple, blue and rose flowers in this manner.

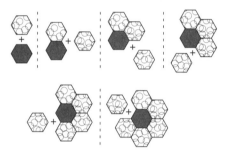

3. Fold stems in half lengthwise and stitch ⅜" from fold. Trim seam allowance to ¹⁄₁₆". Press.

4. Arrange flowers, stems and leaves on background following placement diagram. Stitch in place using slipstitches or invisible machine appliqué stitches.

5. From wrong side, cut out background fabric behind flowers and leaves about ¼" inside stitching line. Remove freezer paper templates.

Traditional Rose

Technique: Machine Appliqué
Templates found on this page.

Cutting

1. Cut one 12½" square from off-white fabric. To trace the appliqué design onto your background fabric, make a pattern as follows: Draw a 12" square on paper and divide the square into quarters. Trace rose and stems with rose in center. Rotate the pattern from the center and trace stems with bud and small flower in each corner. Trace this design onto your fabric.

2. Trace patterns for appliqué pieces onto paper-backed fusible web adding ⅛" to all edges that will be overlapped. Make 4 outer petals, 1 center petals, 1 rose center, 4 inner petals, 20 leaves, 4 rose buds, 4 calyxes, 4 small flowers and 4 small centers. Cut out all pieces.

3. Fuse outer petals to dusty pink, center petals to pink print, inner petals to purple and rose center to light pink. Fuse small flowers to blue, rose buds to purple and calyxes to teal green. Fuse 4 leaves to teal green, 4 leaves to light green and 12 leaves to dusty green. Cut out all pieces.

Directions

1. Fuse outer petals, small flowers, rosebuds, and leaves to position on background (A). Fuse middle petals, and calyxes to position (B). Fuse rose center (C). Fuse inner petals around rose center (D).

2. Using matching thread zigzag around appliqué pieces. Zigzag stitch along stems using dusty green thread.

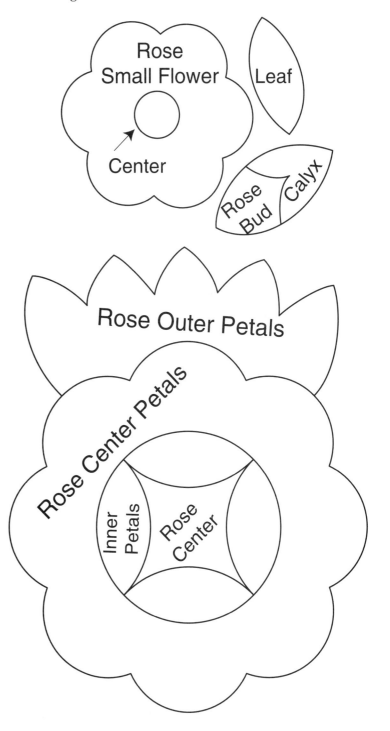

Log Cabin Flower

Technique: Patchwork Log Cabin
Templates found on page 26.

Cutting

1. Make templates for pattern pieces.

2. From off white, cut eight (A) triangles and 4 (D) triangles.

3. Cut 4 leaf sections (B) from dusty green. Cut 4 leaf sections (C) from teal green.

4. Cut 4 petals (E) from dusty pink.

5. Cut center (F) from rose.

6. For log cabin strips, cut 1½" wide strips as follows: From light pink, cut strip (G) 6½" long and strip (H) 7½" long. From light green, cut strip (I) 7½" long and strip (J) 8½" long. From pink print, cut strip (K) 8½" long and strip (L) 9½" long. From multicolored floral print, cut strip (M) 9½" long and strip (N) 10½" long. From rose floral print, cut (O) 10½" long and (P) 11½" long. From green print, cut (Q) 11½" long and (R) 12½" long.

Directions

1. Stitch l triangle (A) to each leaf section (B). Stitch 1 triangle (A) to each petal (E).

2. Stitch 1 triangle (D) to each leaf section (C).

3. Stitch (C-D) units to ends of petal (E-A).

4. Stitch (A-B) units to side (C-E) to form a rectangle.

5. Stitch center (F) to edge of one petal section of rectangle, stitching only half of the seam. Add second rectangle section, then third and fourth. Finish seam of first rectangle.

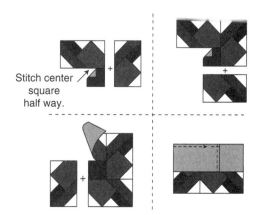

Stitch center
square
half way.

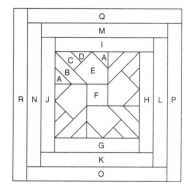 

6. Stitch log cabin strips to the center flower in alphabetical order following the sequence below. Press seams toward the strips.

14

Nine Patch Flowers

Technique: Paper Piecing
Templates found on page 31.

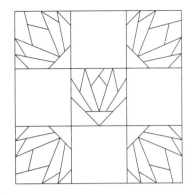

Directions

1. Trace 4 corner flower patterns and 1 center flower pattern to paper.

2. Since many of the shapes on the flowers are about 1" wide, cut 1½" wide strips of purple, purple floral print, blue and light green. Cut teal and light green triangles to cover triangular shapes on patterns.

3. Cut a diamond shape from rose that is ⅛" larger than shape 1 on blocks. With traced side of block up, place diamond right side down under section 1 on paper pattern. Hold paper up to light to be sure it is aligned. If desired, pin in place.

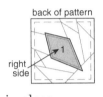

4. Cut a piece from light green strip large enough to cover section 2. Then place under diamond section, with right sides together allowing for seam allowance when stitched.

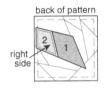

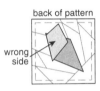

    Holding it in place, turn pattern over and stitch along line between sections 1 and 2. Fold and finger press light green fabric over section 2. Trim fabric so it is about ⅛" larger than shape on raw edges. **Continue piecing the sections in numerical order in this manner.**

5. Cut a piece of light green strip to cover section 3 and place it wrong side up along edge of section 1-2. Holding it in place, turn pattern over and stitch along line between sections 1-2 and 3. Fold and finger press light green fabric over section 3. Trim fabric so it is about ⅛" larger than shape on raw edges.

6. Cut a piece of purple floral print for section 4 and place it wrong side up along side edge of 1-2. Holding it in place, turn pattern over and stitch along line between sections 1-2 and 3. Fold and finger press purple floral fabric over section 4. Trim fabric so it is about ⅛" larger than shape on raw edges. Repeat for section 5.

7. Cut a piece of light green for section 6 and place it wrong side up along end of section 4. Holding it in place, turn pattern over and stitch along line

between sections 4 and 6. Fold and finger press purple floral fabric over section 6. Trim fabric so it is about ⅛" larger than shape on raw edges. Repeat for section 7.

8. Cut a piece of purple for section 8 (use blue for center flower) and place it wrong side up along side edge of 4-6. Holding it in place, turn pattern over and stitch along line between sections 4-6 and 8. Fold and finger press purple floral fabric over section 8. Trim fabric so it is about ⅛" larger than shape on raw edges. Repeat for section 9.

9. For corner flowers, cut a piece of light green for section 10 and place it wrong side up along end of section 8. Holding it in place, turn pattern over and stitch along line between sections 8 and 10. Fold and finger press purple floral fabric over section 10. Trim fabric so it is about ⅛" larger than shape on raw edges. Repeat for section 11.

10. For corner flowers, place long edge of teal triangles wrong side up under seam line of corner triangle and stitch along seam. Fold and finger press teal fabric over section 12.

11. For center flower, place long edge of teal triangle wrong side up under seam line at lower edge of petals and stitch along seam. Fold and finger press teal fabric over section 10.

12. For center flower, place long edge of light green triangles wrong side up under seam line of corner triangles and stitch along seam. Fold and finger press teal fabric over section 11 and 12.

13. Press each flower with an iron. Remove paper from wrong side, carefully tearing it along the perforations made by the stitching.

14. Cut four 4½" blue floral squares. Arrange and stitch the block together.

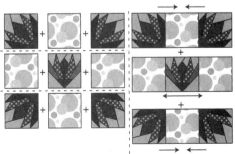

    Press seams in directions of arrows.

15

Tulip Basket

Technique: Machine Piecing; Appliqué
Templates are found on page 29.

Cutting

1. From off white fabric, cut two side sections (A) and one 12½" x 6½" rectangle. Trace tulips, stems and leaves to center of lower edge of rectangle.

2. Cut 6 triangles (B) from pink floral print. Cut 5 triangles (B) from light green. Cut 5 triangles (B) and 1 square (C) from green multicolored floral print.

3. Trace 3 tulips and 2 leaves to paper-backed fusible web. Fuse 2 tulips to dusty pink fabric and 1 tulip to purple fabric. Fuse stems to dusty green.

4. From teal cut one 1" x 8" bias strip. From dusty green cut one 1" x 4" bias strip. Fold stems in half lengthwise and stitch ¼" from fold. Trim seam allowance to ¹⁄₁₆". Press.

Directions

1. Stitch 3 floral print triangles to a light green triangle to make a square unit. Stitch 2 floral print triangles to a pink print triangle to make a square unit. Following piecing diagram, stitch triangle and square units together in rows, then stitch the rows together.

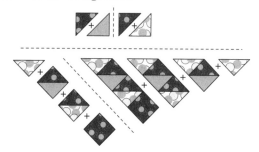

2. Stitch light green triangles to edge of side section to make two large triangles.

3. Stitch side section units to pieced basket.

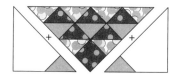

4. Fuse leaves to position on rectangle. Zigzag stitch along the edges using matching thread.

5. Slipstitch teal stem to center line on rectangle. Cut dusty green stem in half and slipstitch to curved stems.

6. Fuse purple tulip to center and pink tulips to curved stems. Zigzag stitch along the edges using matching thread.

7. Stitch rectangle with tulips to top of basket.

Iris

Technique: Machine Piecing
Templates found on page 28.

Cutting

1. Make templates for pattern pieces.

2. From off white, cut 11 small triangles (A), 1 section (B), 3 large triangles (C), 2 small rectangles (J) and 2 large 3½" by 5" rectangles (H).

3. From lavender, cut 4 small triangles (A), 1 large triangle (C), 1 square (D), and 2 upper petals (G).

4. From purple floral print, cut 3 small triangles (A) and 1 medium triangle (E).

5. From gold print, cut 3 medium triangles (E).

6. From purple print, cut 1 center petal (F), 2 small triangles (A), and 2 side petals (I).

7. From green print, cut 1 medium triangle (E) and 1 large triangle (C).

8. From dusty green, cut 1 small triangle (A) and 1 medium triangle (E).

Directions

1. Following piecing diagram, stitch lavender (A) and (C) triangles to matching edges of section (B).

2. Stitch a purple floral print small triangle (A) to a lavender small triangle (A) to make a square. Stitch a lavender square (D) to this square. Join to step 1.

3. Stitch lavender small triangles (A) to short edges of one purple floral medium triangle (E) to form a rectangle. Join to step 2.

4. Stitch purple print small triangles (A) to short edges of one gold medium triangle (E) to form a rectangle. Join to step 3.

5. Stitch one white and one green small triangle (A) to edges of center petal (F). Stitch to step 4.

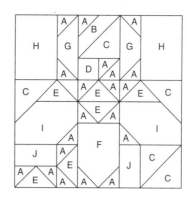

6. Stitch off white small triangles to edges of upper petals (G). Stitch to large rectangles (H). Be sure to make a left and right side.

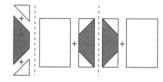

7. Stitch a purple floral small triangle (A) to edge of a gold medium triangle (E). Stitch this piece to the upper edge of the side petal (I). Join a small off-white triangle (A) and a large off white triangle (C) to the edges to form a rectangle. Join to step 6. Repeat, reversing pieces.

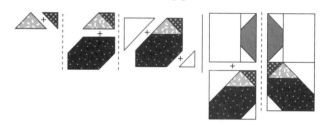

8. Stitch off white triangles (A), to medium green print triangle (E). Join rectangle (J) to top. Stitch off white triangles (A) to dusty green triangle (E). Stitch to previous piece. Attach to step 7.

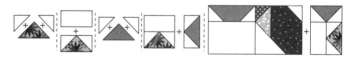

9. Stitch a green print large triangle (C) to an off white large triangle (C). Stitch a rectangle (J) to one side of this unit. Join this rectangle to lower edge of right side strip.

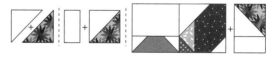

10. Join side strips to center strip to form iris, matching seams.

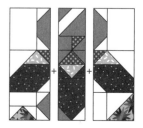

17

Wreath

Technique: Appliqué; Yo-Yo's
Templates found on page 28.

Cutting

1. Cut a 12½" square from off white. Trace pattern for appliqué to each corner. Refer to Urn block on page 10 for more detailed instructions.

2. Trace 16 leaves and 4 bud calyxes to freezer paper. Cut out shapes. Pin paper leaves to dusty green, shiny side up, and cut out fabric ³⁄₁₆" larger than paper. Pin calyxes to teal, shiny side up and cut out fabric ³⁄₁₆" larger than paper. Place leaves and calyxes, paper side up, on ironing board. Carefully press seam allowance over edge of paper one side at a time. Clip to inner point on calyxes. Seam allowance of fabric will stick to the waxy side of the paper eliminating the need to baste under edges.

3. Cut two 1" x 10" bias strips from dusty green for stems.

4. Cut 4 buds from dusty pink.

5. Cut four 4" diameter circles for yo-yo flowers.

Directions

1. To trace the appliqué design onto your background fabric, make a pattern as follows: Draw a 12" square on paper and divide the square into quarters. Trace wreath pattern to each quarter of pattern. Trace this design onto your fabric.

2. Fold stems in half lengthwise and stitch ¼" from fold. Trim seam allowance to ¹⁄₁₆". Press. Slipstitch 10" stems to position on block placing ends under top and bottom flower positions.

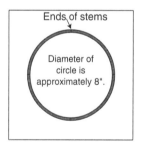

Ends of stems

Diameter of circle is approximately 8".

3. Turn under ⅛" along curved edges of bud and baste. Make a row of gathering stitches along straight edge. Pin bud to background and gather lower edge.

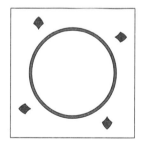

4. Pin calyxes over end of bud. Slipstitch edges of bud in place. Slipstitch or set machine on blind hem stitch and stitch calyxes in place using invisible machine appliqué.

5. Pin leaves around wreath. Slipstitch or set machine on blind hem stitch and stitch in place using invisible machine appliqué.

6. Turn under scant ¼" around edge of circles and

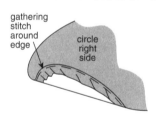

gathering stitch around edge

circle right side

make a row of gathering stitches around edge. Pull up gathers and knot to form yo-yo.

7. Arrange yo-yo flowers around wreath. Slipstitch in place around edges. Sew buttons to centers of flowers.

8. From wrong side, cut out background fabric behind calyxes and leaves about ⅛" inside stitching line. Remove freezer paper templates.

Stained Glass Flowers

Technique: Stained Glass
Templates found on page 32 and on this page.

Cutting

1. Cut one 12½" square of blue floral print. Cut one 10" square of light blue. Using curved template, mark curve in corners of small square. Cut away corners. Trace stained glass design to light blue piece.

2. Trace daffodil petals, daffodil center, tulip, tulip center, flower, flower center and leaves in reverse to paper-backed fusible webbing. Fuse daffodil petals to light yellow, daffodil center to gold print, tulip to rose, tulip center to dusty pink, flower to purple, center to purple print, leave 1 to dusty green and remaining leaves to teal green. Cut out shapes.

3. From black fabric, cut seven l" x 25" bias strips.

Directions

1. Place light blue shape in center of blue floral square. Baste in place along edges. Trim floral fabric from center ¼" inside stitching.

2. Fuse leaves and flowers to position on light blue center.

3. To make leading for stained glass, fold black bias strips in half lengthwise and stitch ¼" from fold. Trim seam allowance to ¹⁄₁₆". Press. (Refer to Urn block on page 10 for detail.)
NOTE: You can pin, baste or simply hold leading

strips in place as you sew. For curved lines, we recommend basting the leading strips. Then sew them in place using invisible machine appliqué stitching (set machine on blind hem stitch). If desired, pin or hold tape in place and slipstitch the edges of the tape to the background.

4. Position leading along the straight lines on background so they overlap edges of flowers and leaves slightly. Sew in place.

5. Stitch leading around leaf number 1. Then stitch leading along stems of flowers.

6. For daffodil, stitch leading around petals beginning at outer edges. Sew center petal last. Sew leading around center.

7. For flower, stitch leading around petals beginning at right side and working left. Sew leading around center.

8. For tulip, stitch leading along edge of center. Then sew leading around tulip beginning at upper center and ending at lower center.

9. Sew leading around leaves in numerical order.

10. Sew leading around edge of light blue center.

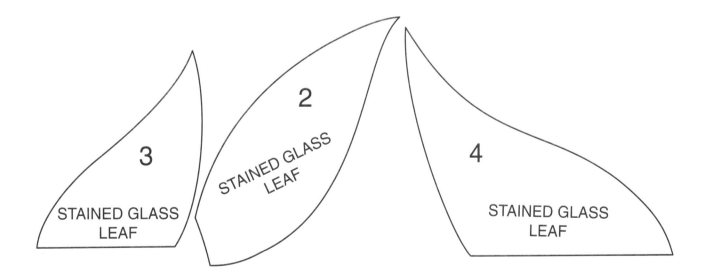

3
STAINED GLASS
LEAF

2
STAINED GLASS
LEAF

4
STAINED GLASS
LEAF

Placemat

Approximate Size: 13½" x 18"

Materials for Two Placemats

NOTE: All fabrics are 45" wide cotton
⅛ yard gold floral print
⅛ yard orange floral print
⅛ yard green floral print
¼ yard small floral print
⅛ yard yellow
⅛ yard maroon
⅛ yard light orange
½ yard bright orange
⅛ yard green
¼ yard black
⅜ yard backing fabric
20" x 28" Poly-fil® Cotton Classic® or Low Loft® quilt batting
8" x 10" piece paper-backed fusible webbing
Thread to match fabrics
Invisible nylon thread for machine appliqué

Cutting

1. Cut four 1½" square centers (A) from maroon.

2. Cut one 1¼" wide strip across the entire width of the following fabrics: gold floral print, orange floral print, yellow and light orange. Cut each strip in half to make strips about 20-22" long.

3. From black, cut one 1½" wide strip and two 1¼" wide strips each across the entire width of fabric. Cut each strip in half to make strips about 20-22" long. Cut 4 each sections (B) and (C) from black. Cut 8 (D) triangles.

4. Cut two 1¼" wide strips from green and two 1¼" wide strips from green floral print. Cut each strip in half to make strips about 20-22" long. Cut four ⅞" x 7½" stems from green.

5. Cut eight 12½" x 1¼" strips from maroon.

6. Cut two 12½" x 8½" center rectangles from small floral print.

Directions for Strip Piecing

1. Arrange yellow and orange solid and floral print strips into two color combinations of 3 strips each as shown in photo on back cover. Stitch each group of 3 strips together. Press seams to one side.

2. From one pieced strip, cut four 2½" wide diamonds at a 45° angle to make the right side of tulip. Reverse 45° angle and cut four 2½" wide diamonds from remaining pieced strip for the left side of the tulip.

3. For the left side of the leaves, stitch a green strip to one edge of 2¼"wide black strip. Then stitch strips to green strip in this order: 1¼" wide black strip, a green floral print strip, 1¼" wide wide black strip and a green strip.

4. For the right side of leaves, stitch a green strip to one edge of 2¼" wide black strip. Then stitch strips to green floral strip in this order: 1¼" wide black strip, a green strip, 1¼" wide black strip and a green floral print strip.

5. Cut four 2¼" wide leaf pieces from the first pieced strip at a 45° angle. Then cut four more pieces at a 45° angle in the opposite direction from the second pieced strip.

Directions for Assembling

1. Assemble tulips, following directions on page 9 for Tulip block.

2. Stitch a maroon strip to each side of each tulip. For each placemat, stitch a tulip to each side of the small floral print center.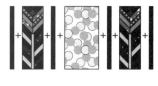

3. Cut two 13½" x 20" pieces from batting and backing fabric. Place backing fabric wrong side up and batting on work surface with placemat centered on top, right side up. Pin and baste layers together. Baste ¼" from outer edge of placemat top.

4. Quilt along lines of tulips, stems, leaves, maroon strips and center.

5. Trim edges of batting and backing around outer edge, ⅜" from basting.

6. Cut 3¼" wide bias strips to make two pieces of binding each 68" long.

7. Make binding and bind edges of placemat following directions on page 6. Use ⅜" seam allowance.

Table Runner

Templates are found on page 29-30.

Materials

NOTE: All fabrics are 45" wide cotton

½ yard large floral or leaf print

⅛ yard gold floral print

⅛ yard orange floral print

½ yard green floral print

⅛ yard small floral print

⅛ yard yellow

¾ yard maroon

⅛ yard light orange

¼ yard bright orange

¼ yard green

½ yard black

⅜ yard backing fabric

24" x 72" piece for backing

24" x 72" Poly-fil® Low Loft® quilt batting

Thread to match fabrics

Invisible nylon thread for machine appliqué

Cutting For Tulip center

1. Cut tulips following directions for Placemat on page 20. Omit steps 5 and 6 of "Cutting."

2. From black, cut a rectangle 12½" x 4½".

Cutting For Tulip baskets (Refer to "Tulip Basket" on page 16.)

1. From black, cut 2 side sections (A) and 2 reversed. Cut two 12½" x 6½" rectangles. Trace tulips, stems and leaves to center of lower edge of rectangles.

2. Cut 12 triangles (B) from light orange, and 10 from maroon. Cut 10 triangles (B) and two squares (C) from small floral print.

3. Trace 6 tulips and 4 leaves to paper-backed fusible web. Fuse 4 tulips to dusty yellow and 2 tulips to bright orange fabric. Fuse leaves to dusty green.

4. From green, cut three 1" x 8" bias strips. Fold stems in half lengthwise and stitch ¼" from fold. Trim seam allowance to 1/16". Press using a bias bar or knitting needle.

Cutting For Sashing and Borders

1. From green floral print, cut a 9⅜" square. Cut the square in half once diagonally to make two triangles. Cut two 2½" x 12½" rectangles.

2. From bright orange, cut two 41" x 1¼" strips, and four 12" x 1¼" strips.

3. From large floral or leaf print, cut two 42" x 4" side borders, two 16" x 4" and two 20" x 4" end borders.

4. Cut 3¼" wide bias strips to piece a binding, 152" long, from maroon.

Directions

1. Make two tulips following directions for Tulip Placemat. Stitch tulips to each side of black rectangle reversing one tulip so that tulip tops point in opposite directions.

2. Make two Tulip Basket blocks following directions on page 16. For patchwork basket, substitute light orange for pink print, small floral print for multicolored floral print and maroon for light green. Substitute yellow tulips for dusty pink tulips and an orange tulip for the purple tulip. Make all stems and leaves green.

3. Stitch green floral print rectangles to ends of tulip block.

   Stitch top edge of tulip basket blocks to remaining edges of rectangles.

   Stitch green print triangles to lower edge of tulip basket blocks.

4. Stitch long bright orange strips to long edges of table runner center. Trim ends diagonally even with edges of triangles.

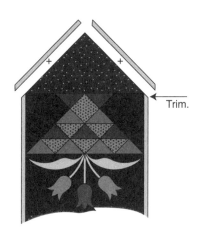

Trim.

   On each end, stitch a short strip to one diagonal edge of triangle and end of orange strip. Trim ends even with triangle and orange strip. Stitch another short strip to remaining edge of triangle and orange strips. Trim ends even with triangle and orange strips.

5. Attach second borders in the same manner as in step 4. Stitch long border pieces to long edges of orange strips. Trim ends diagonally even with edges of triangles.

   On each end, stitch a 16" end border to one diagonal edge of triangle and end of side border. Trim ends even with triangle and side border. Stitch a 20" end border to remaining edge. Trim ends even with side and end borders.

6. Place backing fabric and batting on work surface with table runner centered on top, right side up. Pin and baste layers together. Baste ⅜" from outer edge of table runner top.

7. Machine quilt around tulips, leaves, baskets, sashing and border strips using invisible thread.

8. Trim batting and backing even with outer edge of top.

9. Make binding and bind edges of table runner following directions on page 6.

Garden Maze Wall Hanging

Approximate Size: 50" x 50"
Templates found on page 27.

Materials

45" wide cotton fabrics

1½ yards green leaf print

⅝ yard light green print

⅝ yard bright floral print

⅓ yard green

1 yard purple

⅛ yard violet

⅛ yard peach

⅛ yard bright pink

3 yards backing fabric

56" x 56" Poly-fil® Low Loft® quilt batting

Thread to match fabrics

Invisible nylon thread for machine appliqué

Cutting

For Lily blocks

1. Make templates for pattern pieces on page 30.

2. Cut 12 small diamonds (A) from each purple, violet, peach and bright pink.

3. From off white, cut 24 small triangles (B), 12 squares (C), 8 rectangles (J) 3½" x 5", and 4 each of pieces (H), (F), and (G).

4. From green leaf print, cut 16 large triangles (D). From green, cut 8 large diamonds (E), four 1" x 8" bias strips, and four 1" x 12" bias strips.

For Sashing

5. Using patterns on page 27, make templates for small triangle (F), small cross (G), large cross (H) and large triangle (I).

6. From bright floral print, cut 24 sashing strips 1¾" by 12½", 9 large cross pieces (H), and 14 small cross pieces (G).

7. From light green floral print, cut 12 strips 12½" by 3½" and 24 small triangles (F).

8. From green leaf print, cut 2 border strips 50" x 5" and two border strips 41" x 5", 4 small triangles (F) and 4 large triangles (I).

9. From purple fabric, cut 3½" wide bias strips to piece a binding that is 206" long.

10. For backing fabric cut a 54" length and remove selvages for center. Then cut two pieces 54" x 6" for sides.

Directions

1. Following directions for lily block on page 7, make four blocks. Make 3 lily squares using 4 diamonds of each purple, violet, peach and bright pink. Arrange the lilies in each block by color as indicated in the photo of the wall hanging on the back cover.

2. With long edges and right sides together, stitch a bright floral sashing strip to each edge of a light green print strip to make 12 sashing strips.

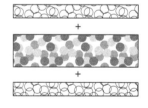

3. To make center connecting square stitch a light green print small triangle (F) to each edge of 2 small cross pieces (G). Stitch (F-G) units to each long edge of large cross pieces (H.

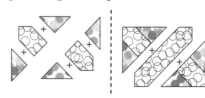

4. To make side connecting squares stitch light green and dark green triangles to small cross piece as shown here. Stitch (F-G) units to one side of four large cross pieces. Stitch (F-G) units to sides of large cross pieces to make four side squares.

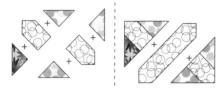

5. To make corner squares stitch a light green print small triangle to each edge of small cross pieces. Stitch (F-G) units to one side of four large cross pieces. Stitch a large green leaf print triangle (D) to remaining side of large cross pieces. Make four corner squares.

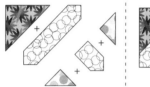

6. Arrange the Lily blocks and sashing strips and squares as shown in Diagram 1 below. Stitch together in rows, then stitch the rows together.

7. Stitch short border strips to opposite edges of wall hanging center. Stitch long border strips to remaining edges. See Diagram 2 below.

8. If not using 72" wide fabric, piece backing fabric as described on page 5.

9. Place backing fabric and batting on work surface with wall hanging centered on top, right side up. Pin and baste layers together. Baste ½" from outer edge of wall hanging top.

10. Machine quilt around lilies, leaves and stems, sashing and border strips using invisible thread.

11. Trim batting and backing even with the outer edge of the top.

12. Make binding and bind edges following directions on page 6.

Diagram 1.

Diagram 2.

Blooming Tote Bag

Approximate Size: 9" x 20"
Templates found on page 31.

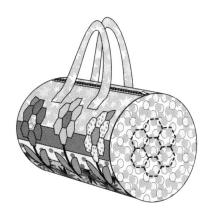

Materials

NOTE: All fabrics are 45" wide cotton

⅜ yard blue print

½ yard light blue print

¼ yard light green floral print

⅛ yard dusty green

¼ yard yellow and green floral print

⅜ yard green print

⅛ yard rose print

⅜ yard yellow star print

⅛ yard bright yellow print

⅛ yard bright green

⅛ yard dark green

1 yard lining fabric

36" x 45" piece Poly-fil® Hi Loft quilt batting

10" x 24" piece Traditional quilt batting

15" x 18" piece paper-backed fusible webbing

2 yards cotton cording

20" light blue heavy duty zipper

Cutting

1. From green print, cut a center section 22" x 9½".

2. From each yellow and green floral print and light green floral print, cut two 22" x 2½" strips.

3. From dusty green, cut two 22" x 2¼" strips.

4. From light blue print, cut two 22" x 6½" top sections and two 24" x 5" handles.

5. To make patterns for tote bag ends, draw a 11" diameter circle (includes ½" seam allowance). Cut two ends from blue print fabric.

6. Cut one rectangle 24" x 36" and two end circles from each tote bag lining and Hi-loft quilt batting. Cut two 24" x 5" handles from traditional quilt batting.

Refer to page 12, "Grandmother's Flowers," to construct the hexagon flowers.

7. Make a hexagon template by tracing the pattern on page 31. Trace 42 hexagons to freezer paper and cut them out. With shiny, waxy side up, pin 4 hexagons to blue print. Pin 14 hexagons to yellow star print. Pin 12 hexagons to each yellow print and rose floral print. Cut out fabric about ³⁄₁₆" from edge of paper.

4. Place hexagons and leaves paper side up on ironing board. Carefully press seam allowance over edge of paper one side at a time. Seam allowance of fabric will stick to the waxy side of the paper eliminating the need to baste under edges.

5. On paper-backed fusible webbing draw 2 stems 5" x ⅜" and four stems 4" x ⅜". Trace 16 large leaves to fusible webbing. Fuse small stems and 4 leaves to bright green. Fuse long stems and 8 leaves to dark green. Fuse 2 leaves to each dusty green and light green print. Cut out stems and leaves.

Directions

1. Stitch yellow and green floral strips to each long edge of green print center section. Stitch green then light green strips to each side of this piece. Stitch light blue top sections to edge of light green print strip.

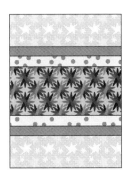

2. Following directions for Grandmother's Flower block on page 12, step 2, make 2 yellow print flowers with blue print centers, 2 yellow star print flowers with blue print centers and 2 rose print flowers with yellow star print centers.

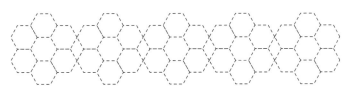

3. Press flowers carefully and remove paper patterns. On each side of background fabric, arrange flowers, stems and leaves following diagram below and pin them in place.

4. Fuse leaves and stems in place. Baste around edges of flowers if desired.

5. Using matching thread, zigzag around each shape.

6. Place lining fabric and batting on work surface with tote bag centered on top right side up. Pin and baste layers together. Baste ½" from outer edge of tote bag top.

7. For tote bag ends, using hexagon template, lightly trace a flower to center of blue print circles for quilting. Place batting between ends and lining right sides out. Pin or baste layers together. Baste ½" from side edges and ¾" from top edges of light blue section.

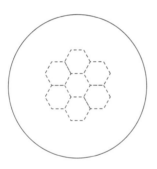

8. Machine quilt around flowers, leaves and stems, and background seams using invisible thread.

9. Trim batting and backing on tote bag even with outer edge of top. Quilt flowers on ends using blue thread.

10. Cut 1½" wide bias strips from yellow star print to cover 2 yards of cording. Stitch bias strip ends together along straight grain. Fold bias strip in half lengthwise and insert cording along fold. Using a zipper foot, baste along edge of cording.

11. Stitch cording around outer edges of ends. Join ends neatly.

12. Trim batting from seam allowance along top edges. Turn under seam allowance along basting. Stitch top edges to each side of zipper.

13. Pin ends to tote bag, clipping seam allowance along side edges of tote bag if necessary. Stitch seam using a zipper foot.

14. Baste quilt batting to handles. Fold handles in half lengthwise with right sides in. Stitch raw edges together leaving an opening in center of long edge for turning. Turn right side out. Slipstitch edges of opening together. Topstitch ¼" from edges.

15. With zipper open, pin then stitch handles to tote bag sides.

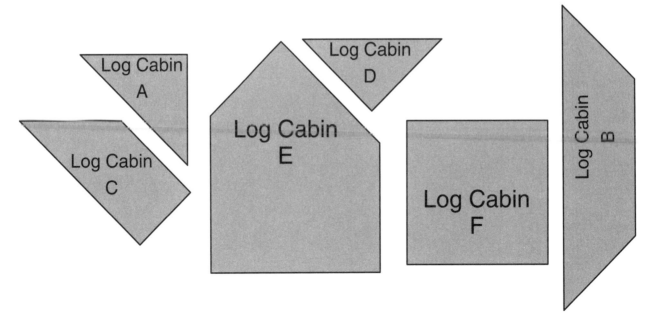

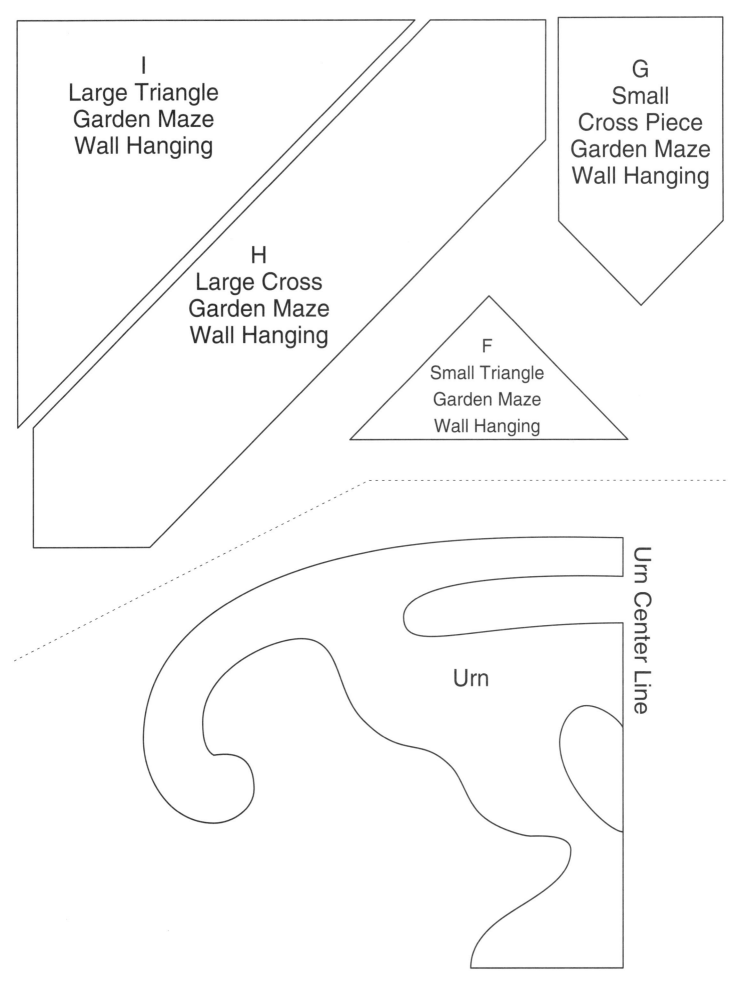

I
Large Triangle
Garden Maze
Wall Hanging

G
Small
Cross Piece
Garden Maze
Wall Hanging

H
Large Cross
Garden Maze
Wall Hanging

F
Small Triangle
Garden Maze
Wall Hanging

Urn

Urn Center Line

27

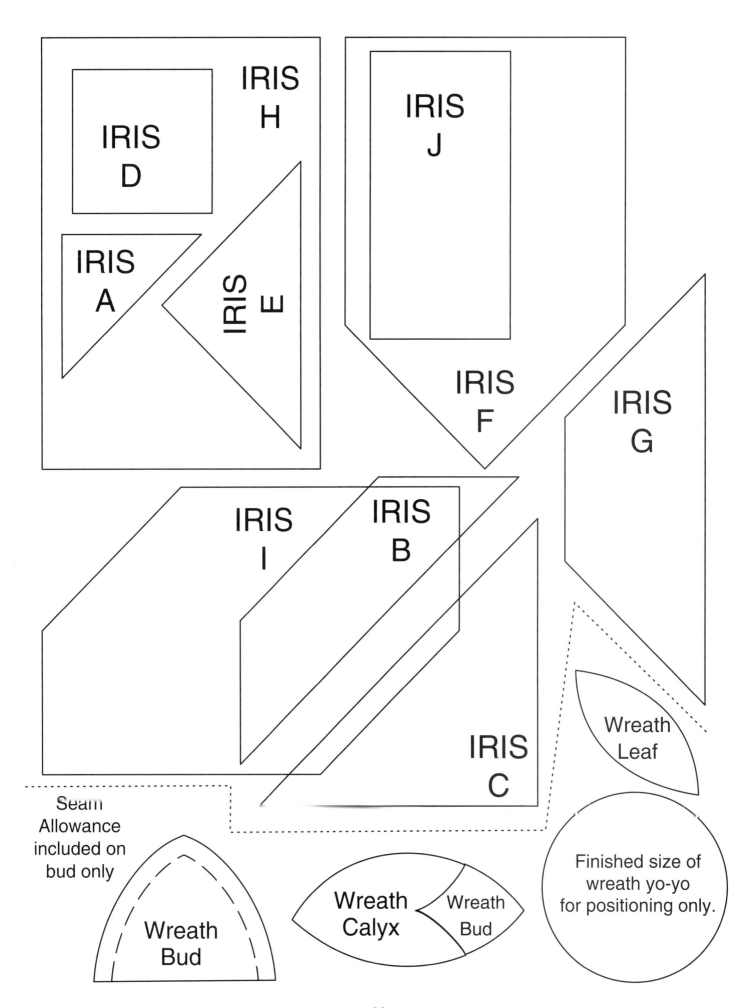

IRIS H

IRIS D

IRIS A

IRIS E

IRIS J

IRIS F

IRIS G

IRIS I

IRIS B

IRIS C

Wreath Leaf

Seam Allowance included on bud only

Wreath Bud

Wreath Calyx

Wreath Bud

Finished size of wreath yo-yo for positioning only.

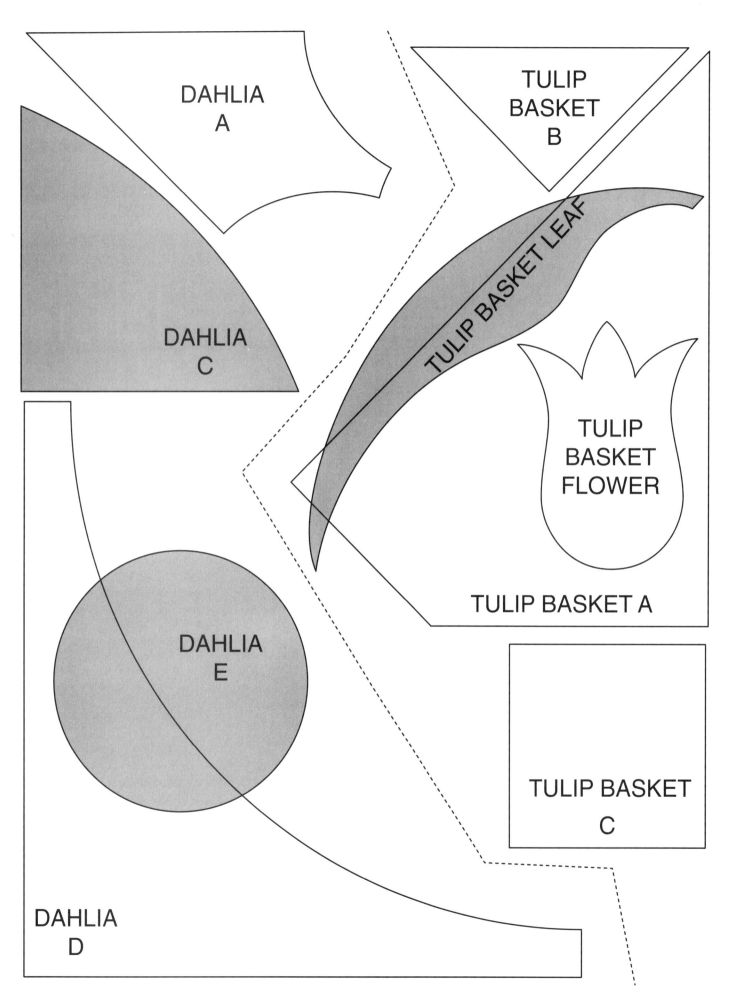

DAHLIA
A

TULIP
BASKET
B

DAHLIA
C

TULIP BASKET LEAF

TULIP
BASKET
FLOWER

TULIP BASKET A

DAHLIA
E

TULIP BASKET
C

DAHLIA
D

29

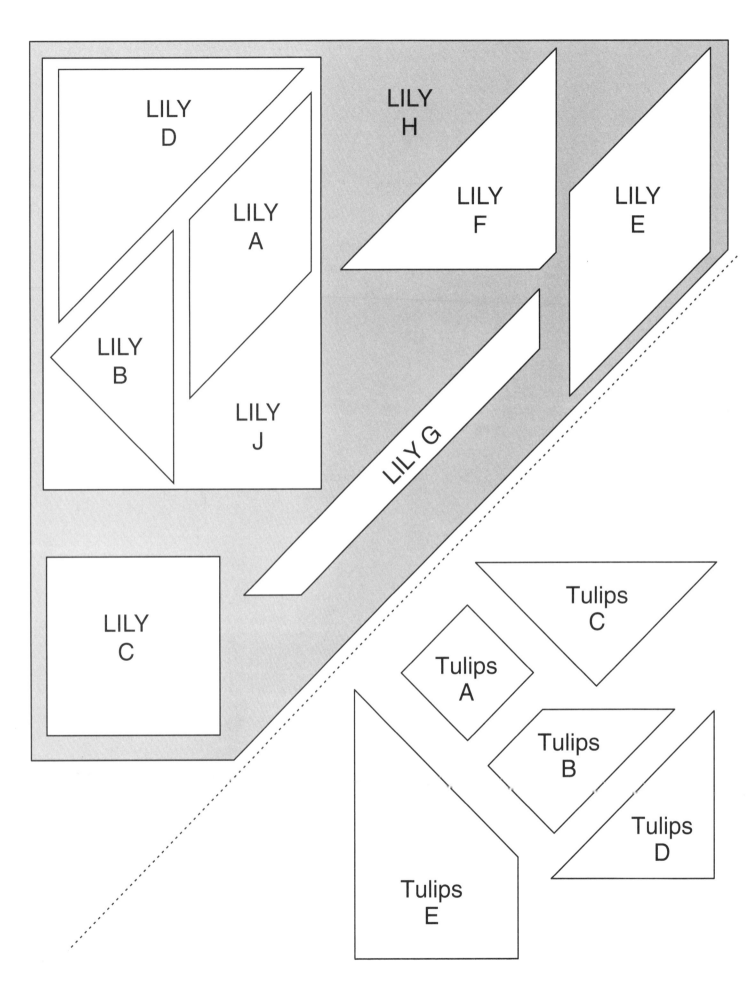

LILY
D

LILY
A

LILY
H

LILY
F

LILY
E

LILY
B

LILY
J

LILY G

LILY
C

Tulips
C

Tulips
A

Tulips
B

Tulips
D

Tulips
E

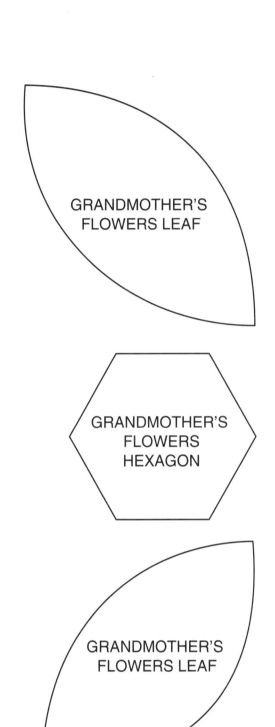

GRANDMOTHER'S
FLOWERS LEAF

GRANDMOTHER'S
FLOWERS
HEXAGON

GRANDMOTHER'S
FLOWERS LEAF

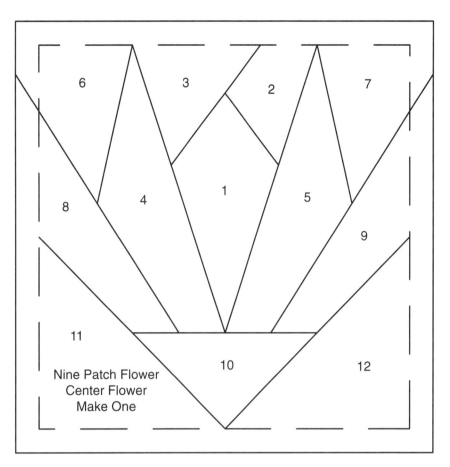

6   3   2   7

8   4   1   5

9

11

10   12

Nine Patch Flower
Center Flower
Make One

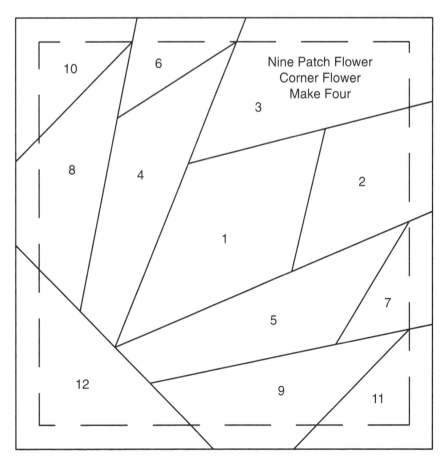

10   6

Nine Patch Flower
Corner Flower
Make Four

3

8   4   2

1

5   7

12   9   11

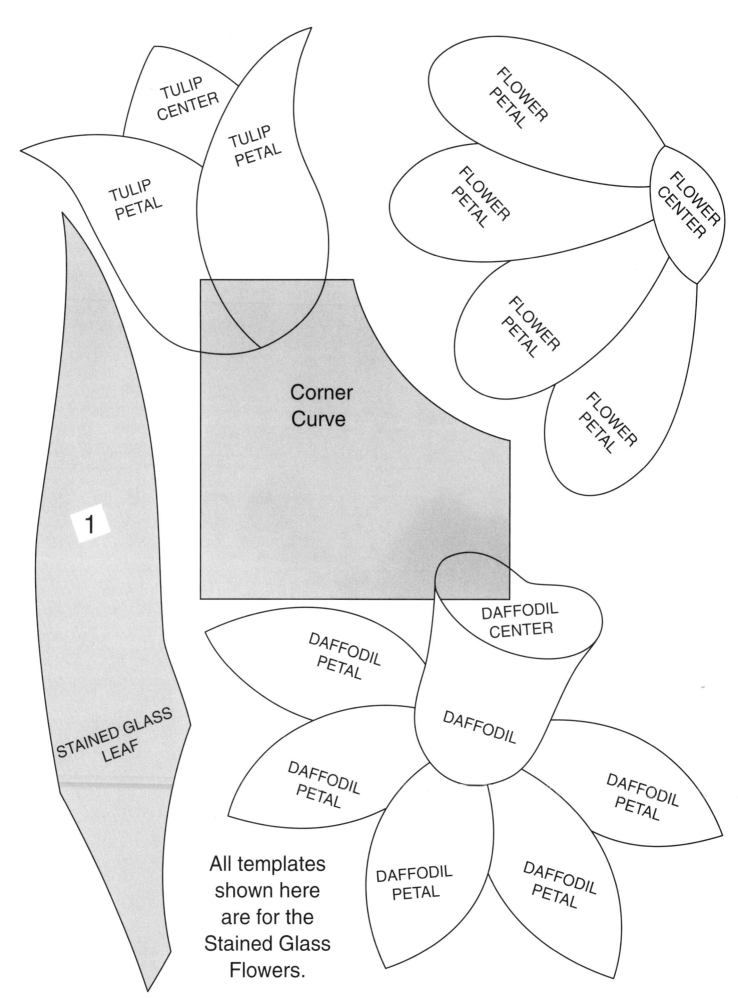

TULIP CENTER

TULIP PETAL

TULIP PETAL

FLOWER PETAL

FLOWER PETAL

FLOWER CENTER

FLOWER PETAL

FLOWER PETAL

Corner Curve

1

STAINED GLASS LEAF

DAFFODIL PETAL

DAFFODIL CENTER

DAFFODIL

DAFFODIL PETAL

DAFFODIL PETAL

DAFFODIL PETAL

DAFFODIL PETAL

DAFFODIL PETAL

All templates shown here are for the Stained Glass Flowers.